Teach Me About
Jesus

L.J. Sattgast & Jan Elkins
Illustrated by Russ Flint

Gold 'n' Honey
BOOKS

for Anna & David _JE

for Caleb & Allison _LJS

TEACH ME ABOUT JESUS

published by Gold'n'Honey Books
a part of the Questar publishing family

© 1994 by Linda Sattgast & Jan Elkins

PRINTED IN HONG KONG

International Standard Book Number: 0-88070-653-X

Most Scripture quotations are from the *Holy Bible, New International Version:*
©1973, 1978, 1984 by International Bible Society;
used by permission of Zondervan Publishing House.

94 95 96 97 98 99 00 01 02 — 10 9 8 7 6 5 4 3 2 1

Contents

A Note to Parents

Since young children are often familiar with many of the stories about Jesus, we have chosen instead to focus on the heart of His teaching so that children will come to know Him even better.

It is our belief that the principles Jesus taught are best learned while children are young and in the process of forming spiritual habits that will affect them for a lifetime.

L.J. Sattgast & Jan Elkins

JESUS TEACHES ME ABOUT

BEING THANKFUL

Sometimes when I get up
the sun is shining.
I get dressed right away
and eat my favorite cereal
for breakfast. I say,
"Thank you God
for such a nice day!"

This is the day the Lord has made;
let us rejoice and be glad in it.
PSALM 118:24

But sometimes it rains,
and wouldn't you know—
my little brother gets the last bowl
of my favorite cereal.
I can fuss and frown,
OR…

I can choose to be thankful.
"Thank you, God,
for a warm, dry house
and plenty of food to eat."

You are my God,
and I will give you thanks;
you are my God, and I will exalt you.
PSALM 118:28

It's easy to be happy
when my dad plays a game
of hide and seek with me.
"Thank you, God,
for such a great dad!"

Every good and perfect gift is from above,
coming down from the Father of the heavenly lights,
who does not change like shifting shadows.
JAMES 1:17

But when Dad says,

"I have work to do,"

I can scowl and complain,

OR…

I can find something else to do.
"Help me to be cheerful
even when I don't feel like it!"

Give thanks in all circumstances,
for this is God's will for you in Christ Jesus.
1 THESSALONIANS 5:18

Most of the time I am nice
to my little brother.
I even let him play
with some of my toy cars.
"Thank you, God,
for my family!"

But sometimes I am mean
to my brother. I push him away
and make him cry. When my mom
makes me sit in the corner,
I can grumble and pout,
OR…

I can say I was wrong.
"Dear God, I'm sorry I was mean.
I'm glad You love me
just as much, even when I do
something wrong."

God is great and strong and kind.
Even when something bad happens,
God can turn it
into something good.

And we know that in all things
God works for the good of those who love him,
who have been called according to his purpose.
ROMANS 8:28

God has given me so much to enjoy.
I want to praise and thank Him
all day long—in everything I say
and everything I do!

I will extol the Lord at all times;
his praise will always be on my lips.
PSALM 34:1

Helpful Hints for Parents about Thankfulness

THE IMPORTANCE OF A THANKFUL HEART

We are not born with character or habits. Character is made and habits are formed. Common, routine, everyday living is the cornerstone of character.

- We are to deliberately deal with self-pity and faithlessness by being thankful in all things (1 Thessalonians 5:16–18).
- A thankful heart brings peace. This peace will guard your mind and heart no matter how disruptive and noisy life gets (Philippians 4:6-7).
- Being thankful is a form of worship that we can choose to do (Psalm 116:17).

KEYS TO A THANKFUL ATTITUDE

It's easy to be thankful when you have success, prosperity, and good health, but until you learn to face, overcome, and use difficulties, you will be vulnerable.

- How do you react under pressure, failure, disappointment, anger, or hurt? Does your child see you working at being thankful and confessing self-pity?
- Do you believe that God is engineering your circumstances? His purpose is for you to know Him and to have a right relationship with Him and others.
- Don't blame God for your depression. Depression means you are demanding an answer now, instead of seeking to know the One who has the answer.
- The only way to put problems in the right perspective is to keep your eyes on Jesus and not give in to self-pity.
- God allows difficult situations but promises to walk through them with you. In the process, He is training and changing you. You are no longer a victim.

WHEN IT'S HARDEST

Your child will experience adverse circumstances where no good can be seen, but it is his or her reaction to the situation that counts.

- Play the GLAD GAME, more commonly known as "counting your blessings." When your child is grumpy or hurt have her find something to be glad about.
- Explain that our enemy, Satan, runs away from praise and thanksgiving.
- To help your child make the right response, carry through with consequences if need be: "We'll work on our project when you choose a happy face."

- Encourage your child to love Jesus for who He is, not for what He gives us.
- When your child whines and grumbles, identify her feelings. Help her deliberately "kick" those feelings out. "Dear God, I'm feeling sorry for myself. Thank you for showing me. Change my heart. Thank you for…"

CAUTION

The things we go through will make us either sweeter and better, or more critical and demanding.

- Consider what you communicate to your child. Are you smiling and praising the Lord at church or with other people, but sour and negative at home?
- When your child is grumpy and ungrateful don't say, "God doesn't like whiny boys." Instead say, "I will be glad to listen when you are not whining."
- Don't give lengthy instructions and try to reason with your child when he is angry and upset. Wait until a cool-down moment.
- No matter what the trouble, nothing can separate your child from God's love (Romans 8:35-39). Don't let trouble come between you and your child either. You will need to forgive him for the emotional upheaval he puts you through.

MORE SUGGESTIONS

A thankful heart and irritation don't mix. There is nothing like thankfulness to get rid of self-pity, defensiveness, and hostility.

- *When your child disobeys:* "I'm glad Jesus doesn't love me less when I do something wrong."
- *When your child has hurt feelings:* "Thank you, God, that I can see my hurt feelings. I choose to forgive."
- *When your child hears some bad news:* "Thank you, God, that you can turn bad things into good things.
- *When your child is angry with a friend:* Ask, "Are you glad to have a friend?"
- *When your child puts herself down:* Say, "How does Jesus feel about you?"

When distressing situations happen, remember: The episode will pass, but your child's reaction will affect the way his or her character is being formed. The circumstances may not even change, but your child will change.

Activities to Reinforce Thankfulness

MY BOOK OF THANKS

- Go through magazines and cut out pictures of things you are thankful for.
- If your child can't find a picture she wants, have her draw one. Even young children can do this, though they may have to tell you what it is.
- Collect snapshots of family and friends whom you love and are thankful for.
- Glue the pictures and photos into a notebook. (You can make your own by folding sheets of blank paper in half and stapling them in the middle.
- Write a title on the cover and decorate it any way you want. Use marker pens, paint, crayons, stickers, etc.
- Keep the notebook in a handy spot where your family can refer to it often.

A GAME OF THANKFULNESS

Play a game with your notebook. For one day (or one week) see how thankful the family can be. If anyone grumbles or complains about anything (including Mom or Dad!) he or she can either read through the entire notebook, or add something new to it.

MEMORY VERSE TO LEARN

Give thanks in all circumstances, for this is God's will for you in Christ Jesus.
(1 Thessalonians 5:17)

JESUS TEACHES ME ABOUT

FAITH

When Keiko's aunt came to visit
she brought her a present.
It was a shiny painted mirror
from Japan.

"Thank you!" said Keiko.
She smiled her brightest smile,
and the girl in the mirror
smiled back.

Keiko played a game
with her mirror.
She turned it this way and that.
"I see you, Mother!" she said.

She turned it again.

"I see you, Chester!"

Chester fluffed his feathers
and chirped.

"Mother, may I go next door
to show Lisa my new mirror?"
"Not right now,"
said Keiko's mother.
"It's almost time for dinner."

Keiko began to pout and whine.
"Look in your mirror,"
said Mother.

This is what Keiko saw.

The girl in the mirror

looked so silly

that Keiko started to laugh.

"I like that face much better,"

said Mother.

"Did you know that *you*
are like a mirror?" asked Mother.

Keiko was surprised.
"How am I like a mirror?"

"Your face shows me
what you are looking at
or thinking about. Just now,
when something nice happened,
you had a happy face.
But what kind of face did you have
when you didn't get your way?"

"Jesus wants you to look at *Him* and believe what *He* says. Then He can change your heart to be more like Him."

"But I can't see Jesus," Keiko said.

And we, who with unveiled faces all reflect the Lord's glory, are being transformed into his likeness…
2 CORINTHIANS 3:18

"One way to look at Jesus,"
said Mother,
"is to read about Him
in the Bible."

"Another way to look at Jesus
is to ask yourself what Jesus
would want you to do."

To this you were called, because Christ suffered for you,
leaving you an example, that you should follow in his steps.
1 PETER 2:21

"What do people see
when they look at *you*?"
asked Mother.

Keiko thought for a moment.
Then she put down her mirror
and ran to the kitchen.

"I want people to see
that I'm looking at Jesus!"
she said.

*Let us fix our eyes on Jesus,
the author and perfecter of our faith…*
HEBREWS 12:2

61

Helpful Hints for Parents about Faith

UNDERSTANDING FAITH
Every child of God has been given a measure of faith (Romans 12:3).
- The foundation of faith is knowing Jesus and being committed to Him.
- Faith is confidence in Jesus. Faith doesn't know and understand everything, but it knows and loves the One who does (Hebrews 11:1).
- Faith is looking at Jesus…developing a habit of being aware of Him…knowing He is with you all the time (2 Corinthians 3:18).
- Faith is not based on reason and intellect. Our reason and intellect can fool us.
- Faith is based on the Word of God (Romans 10:17). The issue is not, "If I could only believe," but rather, "*Will* I believe?"

YOUR ATTITUDE ABOUT FAITH
Are you focused on yourself? Your work? Your experience? If you are not focused on God you will have no power when the going gets tough.
- You are here to know God, not for self-realization.
- Remember, God is always present and in control behind every circumstance.
- Focus on knowing Him, more than trying to find out where He is leading.
- Regularly attend a church where you will be taught the Word of God and learn the heart of God.
- Admit wrong doing and wrong thinking. "The pure in heart will see God" (Matthew 5:8).

FAITH-BUILDERS
- You can't give faith to your child, but you can make her hungry for what you have. Live what you teach. Believe for your child when she cannot.
- When you pray with your child, emphasize the purpose of prayer—to discern the mind and heart of God, not the answer to her prayers. For example: "Jesus, you don't want anyone to be lost. Please save my friend."
- Help your child form the habit of finding out what God says and then acting in faith immediately. For example: "What did Jesus say about forgiving? How about forgiving and blessing your brother right now?"

HOW CAN YOU TELL FAITH IS FORMING?

- When your child desires to know God, he is seeing Him.
- When your child hears, believes, and acts on God's Word, he is seeing Him.
- When your child instinctively turns to Jesus in a crisis, he is seeing Him.
- When your child does wrong and confesses, he is seeing Him.

KNOWING THE HEART OF GOD

We say "It can't be done," because we are not looking at Jesus. Help your child process the fact that faith is not dependent upon feelings or blessings, common sense or reason.

- *When your child is afraid of the dark:* Say, "Even if you feel alone, it's not true. Jesus is with you all the time."
- *When your child is hurt and angry:* Say, "Does Jesus know how you feel? What did He do when someone hurt Him? What is something you could do?"
- *When your child has disobeyed:* After a cool-down period, say, "Why is it important to obey me? Is it because I want the best for you?"
- *When something goes wrong:* Ask, "Does God know about this? Is He still in charge? What can I do that would please Him now?"

CAUTION

Sin is not always the greatest enemy of our faith in God. As has often been said, "the good is always the enemy of the best."

- Do needs, wants, and activities keep you and your family from seeing Jesus?
- If you lose sight of God, you will stop praying and begin to act on your own.
- When God says something, it is easy to argue and debate with Him. Self-consideration (what *I* want, what feels comfortable to *me*) will stop belief.
- Faith is killed by worry. Worry says we don't think God can look after us. (Often we just won't believe because we prefer to worry.)
- Watch out for the attitude, "I will not trust what I cannot see."
- Be careful of building your faith on experience. No matter what changes God has done in you, rely only on Jesus Christ, not on your experiences.

Activities to Reinforce Faith

FAITH MIRROR

- Out of cardboard, cut the shape of Keiko's mirror. (To make it sturdier, cut two mirror shapes and paste them together.)
- Let your child decorate the back of the "mirror."

Try these possibilities:

- Paint the entire surface with one color of poster paint before decorating.
- Cut petals and leaves out of construction paper and make flower designs.
- Cut out a variety of shapes and do an abstract design.
- Make a design with glue, then sprinkle with glitter.

FINISHING THE MIRROR

- Glue a picture of Jesus on the front of the mirror. This can be obtained from Sunday school papers, an old picture book, a poster, greeting card, etc.
- To make the edges look finished, cover them with electrical or masking tape.
- Since we reflect what we look at, use the mirror to remind your child to look at Jesus instead of circumstances.

MEMORY VERSE TO LEARN

Let us fix our eyes on Jesus, the author and perfecter of our faith.
(Hebrews 12:2)

JESUS TEACHES ME ABOUT

FORGIVENESS

Jordan wanted to plant a garden.
He had five packets of seed
and all the tools he needed.
He also had something
he *didn't* need…

A patch of ground full of rocks.

But Jordan planted his seeds
anyway.

Jordan's garden
did not grow very well.
"Looks like you need some help,"
said Grandpa.
Together they dug up the rocks
and threw them out one by one.

When the ground was ready
they planted and watered
the seeds.

Do you think
Jordan's garden grew?

Yes, it did!

There were enough flowers to

share with friends and neighbors.

Grandpa sat Jordan on his knee.
"There's another kind of rock
that needs to be thrown out,"
he said.

"What is it, Grandpa?"
asked Jordan.

"All our hurt feelings
are like rocks in a garden,"
Grandpa replied.
"Our feelings get hurt
when someone calls us stupid."

81

"Our feelings get hurt
when someone pushes us
and we fall down
and skin our knee."

"Our feelings get hurt
when it's our turn
and someone else gets to go first."

"How do I get rid of *those* kinds
of rocks, Grandpa?"
asked Jordan.

"Jesus will help you.
Tell Jesus how you feel.
He understands
because He was hurt, too."

He was despised and rejected by men,
a man of sorrows, and familiar with suffering.
ISAIAH 53:3

"Do you know what Jesus did
when He was hurt?
He said, 'I forgive you'
to the people who hurt Him."

*Jesus said, "Father, forgive them,
for they do not know what they are doing."*
LUKE 23:34

"When we forgive the people who hurt us, it is like getting rid of the rocks in our garden."

For if you forgive men when they sin against you, your heavenly Father will also forgive you.
MATTHEW 6:14

"Then God can grow something good in *me*—can't He, Grandpa?" asked Jordan.

"Yep," said Grandpa, "He *can!*"

But what was sown on good soil is the man
who hears the word and understands it.
He produces a crop, yielding a hundred,
sixty or thirty times what was sown.
MATTHEW 13:23

Helpful Hints for Parents about Forgiveness

PRINCIPLES OF FORGIVENESS

- Forgiveness is not an option. The Bible commands us to forgive (Ephesians 4:31-32).
- We can't receive God's forgiveness if we don't forgive others (Mark 11:25).
- Unforgiveness will hinder our communion with God and block the flow of His grace in our lives (1 John 4:8).
- If we criticize others, it is often because we have the same fault (Romans 2:1).
- How many times should we forgive the same offense? "Seventy-seven times," said Jesus — in other words, as often as the offense occurs (Matthew 18:21-35).
- The Bible tells us to pray for our enemies and to bless them (Matthew 5:44).

YOUR ATTITUDE ABOUT FORGIVENESS

How do you choose to respond to unpleasant situations?

- Ask the Holy Spirit to search your heart and expose hidden resentment.
- Confess anger and bitterness as sin, and ask God for help and healing.
- Exhibit the life of Jesus when you have been insulted. Carefully choose words that edify when you speak about and to other people.
- Forgiveness is not saying sin is okay. Forgiveness brings restoration.
- Admit to your child when you are wrong: "I'm sorry for losing my temper. Will you forgive me?" Pray together.
- Forgive your child. Say, "I forgive you for acting the way you did."

TEACHING YOUR CHILD TO FORGIVE

Teach your child that forgiveness is a choice, not a feeling. He or she can:

- Choose to speak a kind word.
- Choose to pray for another child who is mean.
- Choose to bless someone, no matter how he feels.
- Choose to forgive over and over for the same offense as long as hurt remains.
- Your child's CHOICE affects his actions (what he says and does), and his ACTIONS will eventually affect his feelings.

PRACTICAL SUGGESTIONS

Explain to your child that such things as injustice, meanness, and ingratitude from others are a test for us. They are opportunities for us to learn how to forgive.

- Help your child look for opportunities to forgive.
- Practice and act out scenarios on how to respond in a hurtful situation.
- Your child may not recognize unforgiveness, so help him or her identify hurt feelings. Ask, "Did my words make you feel badly?"
- Have your child acknowledge hurt feelings and ask God to heal them. "Dear God, I feel badly. Thank you for showing me where I hurt inside. I choose to forgive. Please heal me." Then pray over your child (James 5:16).
- Teach your child to forgive quickly. Explain that unforgiveness is like a poison that needs to be removed or it will be harmful to him and others.
- When your child has been wronged and says, "It's not fair!" teach him to not always expect fairness. Tell him that it's more important for him to be fair.
- Help your child find creative ways to "return good for evil."
- Explain to your child that if his attitude doesn't change, it is because he doesn't want to change, or doesn't believe God can change him.
- When it is your child who is in the wrong, he needs to ask forgiveness from the one he has offended.

CAUTION

Anger is expressed outwardly as rage and indignation, or inwardly as resentment and bitterness.

- Don't ignore or minimize your child's feelings; but once they have been identified and acknowledged, help her move on to forgiveness.
- Don't demand that your child forgive. She may need to cool down or count to ten before she's ready to forgive. Help her make the right choice by explaining the consequences of anger.
- Your child cannot experience (understand) God's love unless he or she learns to forgive.
- Never give up on forgiving your child or anyone else. (Think of where *you* would be without the grace and forgiveness of God!)

Activities to Reinforce Forgiveness

MAKE A FORGIVENESS ROCK

- For each family member, collect a rock about the size of a potato.
- Wash and dry the rocks, then paint them any way you wish—the more unique the better. (Poster paint works well.)
- When the paint is dry, write the word "Forgive" on the rock. Use a felt pen, or try fabric paint for a raised look.
- Decide together on the best places to display the rocks—places where the rocks will most often remind your family to forgive.

Optional: To make a paperweight out of the rock, glue a piece of felt to the bottom. Use tacky (thick) glue to make the felt stick.

ROCK HUNT

- Hide some rocks in a room. Make some of them easy to find and others more difficult.

- Let your child hunt for them. When he has searched long enough, show him the location of the remaining rocks.

- Explain that our hurt feelings are like the rocks. Some are easy to see but others aren't. God can show us if we still have hurt feelings we need to forgive.

MEMORY VERSE TO LEARN

Forgive as the Lord forgave you.
(Colossians 3:13)

JESUS TEACHES ME ABOUT

WALKING IN THE LIGHT

(CONFESSION & REPENTANCE)

Gwendolyn wore her best dress
for Patsy's birthday party.
"Be careful with the present,"
said Mother. "And remember
to stay on the path."

Gwendolyn skipped along
until she saw blackberry bushes
on a hillside above the path.
How Gwendolyn loved blackberries!

I won't be long, thought Gwendolyn.
She ran quickly to the bushes
and began filling her mouth
with fat, juicy berries.

105

Just then, Gwendolyn heard

a noise in the thicket.

Was it a wild animal?

Gwendolyn tried to run,

but she tripped on a root.

It was only a friendly dog
coming to say hello.
"Ohhh!" wailed Gwendolyn.
"Look at the present!
And look at my clothes!"

At the party,
Patsy's mother put medicine
on Gwendolyn's scratches.
And she said she could mend
the broken teapot.

Everyone had a good time—
except for Gwendolyn.
What would she tell Mother
about her torn dress?

She could try to hide
what she did.

*I picked some roses
in Patsy's garden.
My dress caught
on the thorns.*

Or she could tell her mother
what really happened,
and ask for forgiveness.

What would Jesus want
Gwendolyn to tell her mother?

*Therefore confess your sins to each other
and pray for each other so that you may be healed.*
JAMES 5:16

*I'm so sorry,
Mother. I disobeyed
and left the path
to pick blackberries.*

Jesus is like a light.

When we obey Jesus,

we walk with Him in the light.

We don't hide anything from Him

and we are best friends.

But if we walk in the light,
as he is in the light,
we have fellowship with one another...
1 JOHN 1:7

When we disobey,
we walk in the dark.
Jesus loves us just as much
and wants to be our friend.
But if we try to hide what we do,
we are not letting Jesus
be our friend.

*If we claim to have fellowship with him
yet walk in the darkness,
we lie and do not live by the truth.*
1 JOHN 1:6

When we tell Jesus
that we are sorry for disobeying,
He *always* forgives us.
Then we can walk
together in the light
and be best friends again!

If we confess our sins,
he is faithful and just and will forgive us our sins
and purify us from all unrighteousness.
1 JOHN 1:9

Helpful Hints for Parents about Walking in the Light

HELPFUL DEFINITIONS

Sin: Missing the mark, like an arrow missing a target. Sin is also like taking a wrong path that twists and turns and leads me in the wrong direction.

- Sin is turning away from God.
- Sin is why Jesus died on the cross.
- Sin is why there is sadness and hurt in this life.
- Sin is like a poison that kills the life of God in me.

Confess: To agree with God that I missed the mark.

Repent: To turn away from sin and do what is right. Get back on the right path. Repentance is more than just remorse and anger at myself. It is a gift from God.

YOUR ATTITUDE ABOUT WALKING IN THE LIGHT

There is no power in the church unless we walk in the Light. Have you decided that sin must *die* — and not just be dismissed, forgotten, or suppressed?

- If I don't admit sin, I will compromise with it.
- When I say, "I must have it at once," I become a slave to that thing.
- When I give in to a habit willingly, that habit begins to dominate me; soon I won't be able to give it up.
- Sin blunts my feelings and clouds my sight until I no longer recognize sin for what it is; over time I will begin to accept sin.
- No human strength can change or stop the consequences of sin.

Can God deliver us from sin?

- If we do not let Him deliver us, we are saying that He cannot.
- The weakest Christian can experience the power of Jesus.
- Ask the Holy Spirit to search you and tell you what is wrong inside. Then confess and repent. (It's important to be accountable to others.)

Caution: Don't become introspective. Get free of the habit of thinking about yourself and what you ought to be. Digging will only bring discouragement and make you focus on yourself. Instead, focus on Jesus and His grace.

TEACHING YOUR CHILD

The "dark" and secret things that are wrong inside will hurt us. Tell your child:

- Jesus wants us to *come to Him*. (Contact with Jesus changes everything!)
- Jesus doesn't want us to wait until we've been good before coming to Him. He wants to take not our goodness, but our sin (which is all we have to give).
- Jesus doesn't love us less when we do wrong; and He doesn't love us more when we do right. We are loved unconditionally.
- Jesus can break every bad habit, every wrong thing.
- Obedience keeps us walking in the Light.

ADDITIONAL COMMENTS

- God does not ask *us* to fix what is wrong inside, because we can't. We need to confess and ask Him to change us.
- The Holy Spirit knows us better than we do ourselves (Psalm 139). Have your child ask the Holy Spirit to show him or her if there is any wrong (sin) inside.
- We can thank Jesus for showing us our sin. Seeing is the beginning of healing.
- Help your child to be accountable. Ask, "What do you think is better—to admit and tell what is wrong, or to be found out?"
- Your child needs to know that it takes courage to admit a wrong. Teach him or her to pray, "Dear God, help me not to be afraid to say I'm wrong."

PRAYER EXAMPLE

Your child can learn to confess sin by repeating phrases after you. For example:

- "Dear God, I agree that telling a lie is wrong."
- "I can't change myself, but you can change me. Wash me clean."
- "Thank you that I can see I was wrong."
- "You always love me just as much, even when I do wrong things."
- "You are so proud of me when I stop hiding and begin to walk in the light."
- "I love you, Jesus."

Activities to Reinforce Walking in the Light

FLASHLIGHT FUN

- After dark, turn out the lights and shine a flashlight. Talk about what it means to walk in the light.

- Let your child hold the flashlight. Think up a list of some examples of attitudes and actions. As you mention each one aloud, have your child turn the flashlight *on* if that attitude or action shows someone who is walking in the light, and *off* if it shows someone who is not walking in the light.

- Each time your child turns the flashlight off, ask him what someone could do to walk in the light again (confess and repent).

PLANT EXPERIMENT

- Grow or purchase two similar potted plants. Place one in a dark closet and leave the other on a sunny window-sill. Continue to water both equally.
- Observe what happens to the plant deprived of light.

Explain to your child that we need to walk in God's light, or we will begin to die spiritually. (Add a reminder again of how we can get back into the light after we have sinned.)

MEMORY VERSE TO LEARN

If we confess our sins, he is faithful and just and will forgive us our sins and purify us from all unrighteousness.

(1 John 1:9)

JESUS TEACHES ME ABOUT

SERVING OTHERS

Two brothers
came to Jesus one day.
"When you become king,"
they said, "we want to have
the two most important jobs.

What do you think Jesus said?

He said,

"If you want to be important,

you must become

a servant like Me.

A servant is a helper,

and I came to help other people."

For even the Son of Man did not come to be served,
but to serve, and to give his life as a ransom for many.
MARK 10:45

Here's how Jesus helped:

He healed sick people.

———

Jesus went throughout Galilee, teaching in their synagogues,
preaching the good news of the kingdom,
and healing every disease and sickness among the people.
MATTHEW 4:23

135

He fed hungry people.

Jesus called his disciples to him and said,
"I have compassion for these people…
I do not want to send them away hungry,
or they may collapse on the way."
MATTHEW 15:32

He washed his friends' dirty feet.

Who else can be a servant?

*He poured water into a basin
and began to wash his disciples' feet…*
JOHN 13:5

Janet is a servant.

How can she help?

Jesus is pleased when we help.

143

David is a servant.

How can he help?

145

Jesus is pleased when we help.

147

Ashley is a servant. How can she help?

Jesus is pleased when we help.

Are you a servant?

How do you help?

Your attitude should be the same as that of Christ Jesus:
Who…made himself nothing,
taking the very nature of a servant…
PHILIPPIANS 2:5-6

153

Helpful Hints for Parents about Serving

UNDERSTANDING SERVICE

Active work and spiritual activity are not always the same thing. Active work may actually be the counterfeit of spiritual work.

- The essential thing is my relationship to Jesus: "That I may know Him" (Philippians 3:8-10).
- In God's eyes, *service* is what we *are* to Him, not what we *do* for Him (Romans 12:1).
- If we want to be of use to God, we must get to know Him. Then we will unconsciously live a life of service (Ephesians 5:1).

YOUR ATTITUDE TOWARD SERVING

- Be ready to do the littlest thing or the great big thing. It makes no difference.
- Real love is shown not just by the spoken word, but by everything we do.
- We do things out of love for Jesus, not out of a sense of duty.
- Serving the Lord is not an impulse, but a deliberate commitment. The weaker you are the more you will see God's mighty power working through you.
- Don't get so caught up in "serving" that it keeps you from hearing God.
- You will teach your child far more from your actions than from your words.

TEACHING YOUR CHILD TO SERVE

Children learn early how to expend energy running after their own needs and fulfillment. An empty life of frustration and dissatisfaction will result.

- Involve your family in special service projects throughout the year, such as donating food to a needy family, helping a sick or elderly neighbor, etc.
- If your child desires to give away one of his toys, let him do it and praise him for it: "I'm glad you like to share."
- Teach your child to tithe as soon as he begins to earn money or receive an allowance.
- Tell your child about the missionaries, charities, and causes you support. Explain why you think it is important to share your money with them.
- A prayer: "Thank you, God, that you are my Father and that I belong to you. How can I serve you?"

CAUTION

Someone once said, "The greatest competition to devotion to Jesus Christ is service for Him."

- It is sometimes easier to teach your child to do the *work* of the Lord than how to *walk* with Him. (If we work for God and get out of touch with Him, we will tire quickly and our love will grow cold.)
- Don't give your child the impression that she is loved and appreciated only when she does what is right.
- Show by your actions that menial work is not beneath your dignity.
- Avoid thinking how useful and valuable you are to God's work.
- We can become so caught up in serving that we don't hear God. Obeying God's will (not meeting the needs of people) should be the deciding factor in where we spend our time and energy.

ADDITIONAL SUGGESTIONS

Helping people is the natural outcome of obedience to God. Teach your child how to serve for the right reasons and how to identify the wrong reasons.

- Encourage your child by saying, "You're such a good helper! Is it because you are learning to have a servant's heart?"
- *When your child doesn't want to help:* Ask, "Why is it important to be a helper?" (Jesus was a servant. We want to be like Him.)
- *When your child refuses to help:* Give him a choice: "You can make your bed and see your cartoon, or you can leave the bed unmade and miss the show." (Make sure you pick a consequence that means a lot to your child, and carry through with it.)
- *When your child does a service and criticizes a sibling for not doing the same:* Ask, "Why do we help others? Is it to be better than someone else, or because someone important is watching? Or is it just because we love Jesus?"
- Good habits take work to form. You can help your child set goals to serve by making a "star chart." When it's filled in, reward him. (God blesses and rewards obedience.)

Activities to Reinforce Serving

THE SERVANT JAR

- On slips of paper write jobs that your child can do, one per paper. Fold up the papers and put them in a large clear jar labeled "Servant Jar."
- Let your child reach into the jar and pick out one paper. Read the task to him and then help him get started. (The element of mystery adds excitement to mundane tasks. Don't be surprised if your child goes enthusiastically from one job to another!)

- Each time your child completes a job put a smiley face on a chart.
- When a predetermined number on the chart is reached, do a special family activity together, like going out for ice cream cones or making popcorn.

Optional: Decorate the jar and lid. Use stickers, or glue on shapes cut out of wrapping paper. A piece of ribbon or lace glued around the lid finishes the job.

SERVANT WEEK

- Pick a week and proclaim it to be your family's "Servant Week."
- Brainstorm for ways you can serve a friend, a neighbor, or a family member.
- Make a list of these ways to serve, and do one a day for a week.
- Try doing some good deeds anonymously.

Optional: Try having a "Servant Month" instead, and do one good deed for someone else every week for a month. You could even mark it on the calendar as a annual event!

MEMORY VERSE TO LEARN

Therefore, as we have opportunity, let us do good to all people, especially to those who belong to the family of believers.
(Galatians 6:10)

Leading Your Child to Christ

Leading a child to Jesus Christ is a tremendous privilege. Even young children can ask Jesus to be their Savior if they :

- Know God loves them.
- Know and agree that they do wrong things.
- Admit without resistance a need for forgiveness.

If your child understands this, the next step is to learn that:

- Jesus died on the cross for my sins.
- God will forgive me, and make me part of His family.

SALVATION PRAYER

Take the time to ask your child questions and clear up any misconceptions. It is best to talk one-on-one rather than in a group setting. Then help your child repeat a prayer, one phrase at a time:

Jesus, I want to become a part of your family.
I want You to be my Savior.
I'm glad you love me.
Wash away all the wrong things I have done.
Thank you for forgiving me.

FOLLOW-UP ON SALVATION

- Have your child tell someone else about his or her decision.
- Read the Bible and pray with your child daily.
- Attend a church that believes in and teaches the Bible.

Excerpted from *Teach Me About God.* If you would like more help
in leading your child to Christ, see the chapter on salvation in *Teach Me About God.*